EVERYONE'S A FOOD CRITIC

52 WEEK
Restaurant Challenge

For
Gastronomes,
Connoisseurs,
Foodies
and
Casual Diners

Dine, Rate & Critique
The Restaurants You Visit

Other Titles in The "Challenge Books" Series:

Everyone's A Critic - 52 Week Movie Challenge
Everyone's A Critic - 52 Week Book Challenge
50 State Travel Challenge

wandering tortoise

ISBN: 978-1696983341

52 Week Restaurant Challenge
Complete The Challenges In Any Order

☑ Food Challenges

☐ 1. A Local Favorite   _____

☐ 2. Your Guilty Indulgence   _____

☐ 3. Restaurant With A View   _____

☐ 4. Ethnic Restaurant   _____

☐ 5. Their Specialty Is Dessert   _____

☐ 6. Nouvelle Cuisine   _____

☐ 7. Coffeehouse   _____

☐ 8. "Farm To Table" Establishment _____

☐ 9. Pho Noodle or Ramen Shop   _____

☐ 10. Newly Established Restaurant _____

☐ 11. Takeout   _____

☐ 12. Has Outdoor Seating   _____

☐ 13. Oldest Restaurant In Your Area _____

☐ 14. Teppanyaki Grill (also called "Hibachi") _____

☐ 15. Their Specialty Is Seafood   _____

☐ 16. Drive-In   _____

☑ Food Challenges

COMPLETION
DATE

☐ 17. Has Live Music   _____

☐ 18. Tapas Bar   _____

☐ 19. Not A Chain Or Franchise   _____

☐ 20. A Place That Always Looks Busy   _____

☐ 21. A Doughnut Shop   _____

☐ 22. Family Style   _____

☐ 23. Buffet   _____

☐ 24. Has A Salad Bar   _____

☐ 25. Their Specialty is Vegetarian or Vegan   _____

☐ 26. A Restaurant With An Interesting History   _____

☐ 27. A Steakhouse   _____

☐ 28. An Ice Cream Parlor   _____

☐ 29. Dinner Theater   _____

☐ 30. A Pizzeria   _____

☐ 31. Fast Casual   _____

☐ 32. Teahouse   _____

☐ 33. A Restaurant You've Been Wanting To Try   _____

☐ 34. Sushi Bar   _____

☑ Food Challenges

☐ 35. Their Specialty Is Bread   ————————

☐ 36. Fine Dining   ————————

☐ 37. A Delicatessen (Deli)   ————————

☐ 38. Named After A Person   ————————

☐ 39. Street Food   ————————

☐ 40. Their Specialty Is Breakfast   ————————

☐ 41. A Bakery   ————————

☐ 42. Combined Food & Activity   ————————

☐ 43. A Great Place For Groups   ————————

☐ 44. A Cafeteria   ————————

☐ 45. Their Specialty is Barbecue   ————————

☐ 46. Pop-Up Restaurant   ————————

☐ 47. A Diner   ————————

☐ 48. A Beer Garden   ————————

☐ 49. Sandwich Shop   ————————

☐ 50. Reservations Recommended   ————————

☐ 51. A Gastropub   ————————

☐ 52. Your Favorite Restaurant   ————————

A Local Favorite

These are usually favorite spots for a reason...
great food, great service, and great atmosphere.
How does your choice stack up to your expectations?

Restaurant Name:_____
_____

Location:_____
_____

How many in your group?_____

Date Completed:

_____

My Overall Rating:

☆☆☆☆☆

What other restaurants did you consider for this challenge?_____
_____

_____

Why did you choose this place over the other possiblities?_____
_____

_____

_____

🍴 Rate The Following

☆☆☆☆☆ Food   ☆☆☆☆☆ Selection

☆☆☆☆☆ Service   ☆☆☆☆☆ Location

☆☆☆☆☆ Cleanliness   ☆☆☆☆☆ Convenience

☆☆☆☆☆ Ambience   ☆☆☆☆☆ Value

What did you order?_____

_____

_____

What other dishes did you consider?_____

_____

_____

Did your order arrive quickly?_____

Were you satisfied with your order? Why or why not?_____

_____

_____

Describe the service you received. Was it fast and friendly? Did

the person helping you seem knowledgable?_____

_____

_____

Describe the atmosphere. Was there anything unique?_____

_____

_____

Would you return to this establishment? Why or why not?_____

_____

_____

Would you like to mention anything else?_____

_____

Your Guilty Indulgence

Do you enjoy the occassional frozen mocha latte?
Are light, flaky pastries your weakness? This is an easy
challenge to tackle, catering to your guilty indulgence.

Restaurant Name:_____

_____

Location:_____

_____

How many in your group?_____

Date Completed:

_____

My Overall Rating:

☆☆☆☆☆

What other restaurants did you consider for this challenge?_____

_____

_____

Why did you choose this place over the other possiblities?_____

_____

_____

_____

🍴 Rate The Following

☆☆☆☆☆ Food   ☆☆☆☆☆ Selection

☆☆☆☆☆ Service   ☆☆☆☆☆ Location

☆☆☆☆☆ Cleanliness   ☆☆☆☆☆ Convenience

☆☆☆☆☆ Ambience   ☆☆☆☆☆ Value

What did you order?_____

_____

_____

What other dishes did you consider?_____

_____

_____

Did your order arrive quickly?_____

Were you satisfied with your order? Why or why not?_____

_____

_____

Describe the service you received. Was it fast and friendly? Did

the person helping you seem knowledgable?_____

_____

_____

Describe the atmosphere. Was there anything unique?_____

_____

_____

Would you return to this establishment? Why or why not?_____

_____

_____

Would you like to mention anything else?_____

_____

_____

Restaurant With A View

Riverside. An ocean pier. A mountain lodge.
High above a city. Choose a restaurant with
a fabulous view to admire while you dine.

Restaurant Name:_____

_____

Location:_____

_____

How many in your group?_____

Date Completed:

_____

My Overall Rating:

☆☆☆☆☆

What other restaurants did you consider for this challenge?_____

_____

_____

Why did you choose this place over the other possiblities?_____

_____

_____

_____

🍴 Rate The Following

☆☆☆☆☆ Food

☆☆☆☆☆ Service

☆☆☆☆☆ Cleanliness

☆☆☆☆☆ Ambience

☆☆☆☆☆ Selection

☆☆☆☆☆ Location

☆☆☆☆☆ Convenience

☆☆☆☆☆ Value

What did you order?_____

_____

_____

What other dishes did you consider?_____

_____

_____

Did your order arrive quickly?_____

Were you satisfied with your order? Why or why not?_____

_____

_____

Describe the service you received. Was it fast and friendly? Did

the person helping you seem knowledgable?_____

_____

_____

Describe the atmosphere. Was there anything unique?_____

_____

_____

Would you return to this establishment? Why or why not?_____

_____

_____

Would you like to mention anything else?_____

_____

_____

Ethnic Restaurant

The top three ethnic foods in the U.S. are Chinese, Mexican, and Italian. Also moving up in popularity are Korean, Indian, and Mediterranean. Choose your favorite or try something new!

Restaurant Name:_____

_____

Location:_____

_____

How many in your group?_____

Date Completed:

_____

My Overall Rating:

☆☆☆☆☆

What other restaurants did you consider for this challenge?_____

_____

_____

Why did you choose this place over the other possiblities?_____

_____

_____

_____

🍴 Rate The Following

☆☆☆☆☆ Food   ☆☆☆☆☆ Selection

☆☆☆☆☆ Service   ☆☆☆☆☆ Location

☆☆☆☆☆ Cleanliness   ☆☆☆☆☆ Convenience

☆☆☆☆☆ Ambience   ☆☆☆☆☆ Value

What did you order?_____

_____

_____

What other dishes did you consider?_____

_____

_____

Did your order arrive quickly?_____

Were you satisfied with your order? Why or why not?_____

_____

_____

Describe the service you received. Was it fast and friendly? Did

the person helping you seem knowledgable?_____

_____

_____

Describe the atmosphere. Was there anything unique?_____

_____

_____

Would you return to this establishment? Why or why not?_____

_____

_____

Would you like to mention anything else?_____

_____

_____

Their Specialty is Dessert

Mmmm...dessert. Choose a place known for their desserts.
You don't even have to order a meal there.
Just stop in for coffee and dessert if you want.

Restaurant Name:_____

_____

Location:_____

_____

How many in your group?_____

Date Completed:

_____

My Overall Rating:

☆☆☆☆☆

What other restaurants did you consider for this challenge?_____

_____

_____

Why did you choose this place over the other possiblities?_____

_____

_____

_____

🍴 Rate The Following

☆☆☆☆☆ Food   ☆☆☆☆☆ Selection

☆☆☆☆☆ Service   ☆☆☆☆☆ Location

☆☆☆☆☆ Cleanliness   ☆☆☆☆☆ Convenience

☆☆☆☆☆ Ambience   ☆☆☆☆☆ Value

What did you order?_____

_____

_____

What other dishes did you consider?_____

_____

_____

Did your order arrive quickly?_____

Were you satisfied with your order? Why or why not?_____

_____

_____

Describe the service you received. Was it fast and friendly? Did

the person helping you seem knowledgable?_____

_____

_____

Describe the atmosphere. Was there anything unique?_____

_____

_____

Would you return to this establishment? Why or why not?____

_____

_____

Would you like to mention anything else?_____

_____

_____

Nouvelle Cuisine

It's all about freshness and presentation (and, of course, taste).
If you've never taken a picture of your food before,
this dining experience might change that.

Restaurant Name:_____

_____

Location:_____

_____

How many in your group?_____

Date Completed:

_____

My Overall Rating:

☆☆☆☆☆

What other restaurants did you consider for this challenge?_____

_____

_____

Why did you choose this place over the other possiblities?_____

_____

_____

_____

🍴 Rate The Following

☆☆☆☆☆ Food   ☆☆☆☆☆ Selection

☆☆☆☆☆ Service   ☆☆☆☆☆ Location

☆☆☆☆☆ Cleanliness   ☆☆☆☆☆ Convenience

☆☆☆☆☆ Ambience   ☆☆☆☆☆ Value

What did you order?_____

_____

_____

What other dishes did you consider?_____

_____

_____

Did your order arrive quickly?_____

Were you satisfied with your order? Why or why not?_____

_____

_____

Describe the service you received. Was it fast and friendly? Did

the person helping you seem knowledgable?_____

_____

_____

Describe the atmosphere. Was there anything unique?_____

_____

_____

Would you return to this establishment? Why or why not?_____

_____

_____

Would you like to mention anything else?_____

_____

_____

A Coffeehouse

Your coffeehouse may offer wifi and a relaxing spot to work, or they may have live music or poetry readings from time to time. Stop in to see what your coffeehouse has to offer.

Restaurant Name:_____

_____

Location:_____

_____

How many in your group?_____

Date Completed:

_____

My Overall Rating:

☆☆☆☆☆

What other restaurants did you consider for this challenge?____

_____

_____

Why did you choose this place over the other possiblities?____

_____

_____

_____

Rate The Following

☆☆☆☆☆ Food

☆☆☆☆☆ Service

☆☆☆☆☆ Cleanliness

☆☆☆☆☆ Ambience

☆☆☆☆☆ Selection

☆☆☆☆☆ Location

☆☆☆☆☆ Convenience

☆☆☆☆☆ Value

What did you order?_____

_____

_____

What other dishes did you consider?_____

_____

_____

Did your order arrive quickly?_____

Were you satisfied with your order? Why or why not?_____

_____

_____

Describe the service you received. Was it fast and friendly? Did

the person helping you seem knowledgable?_____

_____

_____

Describe the atmosphere. Was there anything unique?_____

_____

_____

Would you return to this establishment? Why or why not?_____

_____

_____

Would you like to mention anything else?_____

_____

_____

"Farm To Table" Establishment

Seasonal ingredients, locally-sourced
directly from farmers, ranchers and fishers,
means fresh, creative dishes and an ever-changing menu.

Restaurant Name:_____

_____

Location:_____

_____

How many in your group?_____

Date Completed:

_____

My Overall Rating:

☆☆☆☆☆

What other restaurants did you consider for this challenge?____

_____

_____

Why did you choose this place over the other possiblities?_____

_____

_____

_____

🍴 Rate The Following

☆☆☆☆☆ Food   ☆☆☆☆☆ Selection

☆☆☆☆☆ Service   ☆☆☆☆☆ Location

☆☆☆☆☆ Cleanliness   ☆☆☆☆☆ Convenience

☆☆☆☆☆ Ambience   ☆☆☆☆☆ Value

What did you order?_____

_____

_____

What other dishes did you consider?_____

_____

_____

Did your order arrive quickly?_____

Were you satisfied with your order? Why or why not?_____

_____

_____

Describe the service you received. Was it fast and friendly? Did

the person helping you seem knowledgable?_____

_____

_____

Describe the atmosphere. Was there anything unique?_____

_____

_____

Would you return to this establishment? Why or why not?____

_____

_____

Would you like to mention anything else?_____

_____

_____

Pho Noodle or Ramen Shop

Join the scores of "pho-natics"
and hopeless "ramen-tics"
that enjoy their noodle bowls regularly.

Restaurant Name:_____

_____

Location:_____

_____

How many in your group?_____

Date Completed:

_____

My Overall Rating:

☆☆☆☆☆

What other restaurants did you consider for this challenge?_____

_____

_____

Why did you choose this place over the other possiblities?_____

_____

_____

_____

Rate The Following

☆☆☆☆☆ Food   ☆☆☆☆☆ Selection

☆☆☆☆☆ Service   ☆☆☆☆☆ Location

☆☆☆☆☆ Cleanliness   ☆☆☆☆☆ Convenience

☆☆☆☆☆ Ambience   ☆☆☆☆☆ Value

What did you order?_____

_____

_____

What other dishes did you consider?_____

_____

_____

Did your order arrive quickly?_____

Were you satisfied with your order? Why or why not?_____

_____

_____

Describe the service you received. Was it fast and friendly? Did

the person helping you seem knowledgable?_____

_____

_____

Describe the atmosphere. Was there anything unique?_____

_____

_____

Would you return to this establishment? Why or why not?_____

_____

_____

Would you like to mention anything else?_____

_____

_____

A Newly Established Restaurant

It's new in town and eager to please.
Give a newly established restaurant a chance.
It might become your new favorite dining spot!

Restaurant Name:_____

_____

Location:_____

_____

How many in your group?_____

Date Completed:

_____

My Overall Rating:

☆☆☆☆☆

What other restaurants did you consider for this challenge?_____

_____

_____

Why did you choose this place over the other possiblities?_____

_____

_____

_____

_____

🍴 Rate The Following

☆☆☆☆☆ Food　　☆☆☆☆☆ Selection

☆☆☆☆☆ Service　　☆☆☆☆☆ Location

☆☆☆☆☆ Cleanliness　　☆☆☆☆☆ Convenience

☆☆☆☆☆ Ambience　　☆☆☆☆☆ Value

What did you order?_____

_____

_____

What other dishes did you consider?_____

_____

_____

Did your order arrive quickly?_____

Were you satisfied with your order? Why or why not?_____

_____

_____

Describe the service you received. Was it fast and friendly? Did
the person helping you seem knowledgable?_____

_____

_____

Describe the atmosphere. Was there anything unique?_____

_____

_____

Would you return to this establishment? Why or why not?_____

_____

_____

Would you like to mention anything else?_____

_____

_____

Takeout

...or take-out, carry-out, or to-go. Call it what you want.
Chinese takeout and pizza might be favorites, but consider
others as well. Mexican, Indian, sushi, sandwiches, breakfast...

Restaurant Name:_____

_____

Location:_____

_____

How many in your group?_____

Date Completed:

_____

My Overall Rating:

☆☆☆☆☆

What other restaurants did you consider for this challenge?_____

_____

_____

Why did you choose this place over the other possiblities?_____

_____

_____

_____

🍴 Rate The Following

☆☆☆☆☆ Food   ☆☆☆☆☆ Selection

☆☆☆☆☆ Service   ☆☆☆☆☆ Location

☆☆☆☆☆ Cleanliness ☆☆☆☆☆ Convenience

☆☆☆☆☆ Ambience   ☆☆☆☆☆ Value

What did you order?_____

_____

_____

What other dishes did you consider?_____

_____

_____

Did your order arrive quickly?_____

Were you satisfied with your order? Why or why not?_____

_____

_____

Describe the service you received. Was it fast and friendly? Did

the person helping you seem knowledgable?_____

_____

_____

Was your food packaged well for takeout? Was it easy to re-

re-heat and eat?_____

_____

Would you return to this establishment? Why or why not?_____

_____

_____

Would you like to mention anything else?_____

_____

_____

Has Outdoor Seating

It doesn't matter if the place you select offers outdoor seating exclusively or if it has only a few tables available on the patio. Just enjoy dining in the fresh air.

Restaurant Name:_____

_____

Location:_____

_____

How many in your group?_____

Date Completed:

_____

My Overall Rating:

☆ ☆ ☆ ☆ ☆

What other restaurants did you consider for this challenge?_____

_____

_____

Why did you choose this place over the other possiblities?_____

_____

_____

_____

Rate The Following

☆☆☆☆☆ Food   ☆☆☆☆☆ Selection

☆☆☆☆☆ Service   ☆☆☆☆☆ Location

☆☆☆☆☆ Cleanliness   ☆☆☆☆☆ Convenience

☆☆☆☆☆ Ambience   ☆☆☆☆☆ Value

What did you order?_____

_____

_____

What other dishes did you consider?_____

_____

_____

Did your order arrive quickly?_____

Were you satisfied with your order? Why or why not?_____

_____

_____

Describe the service you received. Was it fast and friendly? Did the person helping you seem knowledgable?_____

_____

_____

Describe the atmosphere. Was there anything unique?_____

_____

_____

Would you return to this establishment? Why or why not?_____

_____

_____

Would you like to mention anything else?_____

_____

_____

Oldest Restaurant In Your Area

Whether it's a tavern from the 1700s or a "Mom & Pop" establishment that has been serving locals for 40 years, enjoy dining at the oldest restaurant in your area

Restaurant Name:_____

_____

Location:_____

_____

How many in your group?_____

Date Completed:

_____

My Overall Rating:

☆☆☆☆☆

What other restaurants did you consider for this challenge?_____

_____

_____

Why did you choose this place over the other possiblities?_____

_____

_____

_____

🍴 Rate The Following

☆☆☆☆☆ Food

☆☆☆☆☆ Service

☆☆☆☆☆ Cleanliness

☆☆☆☆☆ Ambience

☆☆☆☆☆ Selection

☆☆☆☆☆ Location

☆☆☆☆☆ Convenience

☆☆☆☆☆ Value

What did you order?_____

_____

_____

What other dishes did you consider?_____

_____

_____

Did your order arrive quickly?_____

Were you satisfied with your order? Why or why not?_____

_____

_____

Describe the service you received. Was it fast and friendly? Did

the person helping you seem knowledgable?_____

_____

_____

Describe the atmosphere. Was there anything unique?_____

_____

_____

Would you return to this establishment? Why or why not?_____

_____

_____

Would you like to mention anything else?_____

_____

_____

Teppanyaki Grill

Gather around a teppanyaki grill (commonly referred to as "hibachi") and enjoy a fantastic show while the chef prepares and serves flavorful Japanese cuisine.

Restaurant Name:_____

_____

Location:_____

_____

How many in your group?_____

Date Completed:

_____

My Overall Rating:

☆☆☆☆☆

What other restaurants did you consider for this challenge?_____

_____

_____

Why did you choose this place over the other possiblities?_____

_____

_____

_____

🍴 Rate The Following

☆☆☆☆☆ Food   ☆☆☆☆☆ Selection

☆☆☆☆☆ Service   ☆☆☆☆☆ Location

☆☆☆☆☆ Cleanliness   ☆☆☆☆☆ Convenience

☆☆☆☆☆ Ambience   ☆☆☆☆☆ Value

What did you order?_____

_____

_____

What other dishes did you consider?_____

_____

_____

Were you satisfied with your order? Why or why not?_____

_____

_____

_____

Describe the service you received. Was it fast and friendly? Did

the person helping you seem knowledgable?_____

_____

_____

Desides teppanyaki, were there other dining options?_____

_____

_____

Would you return to this establishment? Why or why not?_____

_____

_____

Would you like to mention anything else?_____

_____

_____

Their Specialty Is Seafood

Choose anything from a family run crab shack
or fish 'n chips operation on a pier to a swanky establishment
with a fully stocked selection of all things seafood.

Restaurant Name:_____

_____

Location:_____

_____

How many in your group?_____

Date Completed:

_____

My Overall Rating:

☆☆☆☆☆

What other restaurants did you consider for this challenge?_____

_____

_____

Why did you choose this place over the other possiblities?_____

_____

_____

_____

Rate The Following

☆☆☆☆☆ Food

☆☆☆☆☆ Service

☆☆☆☆☆ Cleanliness

☆☆☆☆☆ Ambience

☆☆☆☆☆ Selection

☆☆☆☆☆ Location

☆☆☆☆☆ Convenience

☆☆☆☆☆ Value

What did you order?_____

_____

_____

What other dishes did you consider?_____

_____

_____

Did your order arrive quickly?_____

Were you satisfied with your order? Why or why not?_____

_____

_____

Describe the service you received. Was it fast and friendly? Did

the person helping you seem knowledgable?_____

_____

_____

Describe the atmosphere. Was there anything unique?_____

_____

_____

Would you return to this establishment? Why or why not?_____

_____

_____

Would you like to mention anything else?_____

_____

_____

Drive-In

The iconic drive-in. Even now you can
find them dotted around the country.
Some still have roller-skating carhops, too!

Restaurant Name:_____

_____

Location:_____

_____

How many in your group?_____

Date Completed:

_____

My Overall Rating:

☆ ☆ ☆ ☆ ☆

What other restaurants did you consider for this challenge?_____

_____

_____

Why did you choose this place over the other possiblities?_____

_____

_____

_____

🍴 Rate The Following

☆☆☆☆☆ Food   ☆☆☆☆☆ Selection

☆☆☆☆☆ Service   ☆☆☆☆☆ Location

☆☆☆☆☆ Cleanliness ☆☆☆☆☆ Convenience

☆☆☆☆☆ Ambience   ☆☆☆☆☆ Value

What did you order?_____

_____

_____

What other dishes did you consider?_____

_____

_____

Did your order arrive quickly?_____

Were you satisfied with your order? Why or why not?_____

_____

_____

Describe the service you received. Was it fast and friendly? Did

the person helping you seem knowledgable?_____

_____

_____

Describe the atmosphere. Was there anything unique?_____

_____

_____

Would you return to this establishment? Why or why not?_____

_____

_____

Would you like to mention anything else?_____

_____

_____

Has Live Music

Find some live music to enjoy while you eat. A jazz bar,
a lone guitarist at your local coffeehouse,
or a street parade where you're surrounded by music and food.

Restaurant Name:_____

_____

Location:_____

_____

How many in your group?_____

Date Completed:

_____

My Overall Rating:

☆☆☆☆☆

What other restaurants did you consider for this challenge?_____

_____

_____

Why did you choose this place over the other possiblities?_____

_____

_____

_____

🍴 Rate The Following

☆☆☆☆☆ Food

☆☆☆☆☆ Service

☆☆☆☆☆ Cleanliness

☆☆☆☆☆ Ambience

☆☆☆☆☆ Selection

☆☆☆☆☆ Location

☆☆☆☆☆ Convenience

☆☆☆☆☆ Value

What did you order?_____

_____

_____

What other dishes did you consider?_____

_____

_____

Did your order arrive quickly?_____

Were you satisfied with your order? Why or why not?_____

_____

_____

Describe the service you received. Was it fast and friendly? Did
the person helping you seem knowledgable?_____

_____

_____

Describe the atmosphere. Was there anything unique?_____

_____

_____

Would you return to this establishment? Why or why not?_____

_____

_____

Would you like to mention anything else?_____

_____

_____

Tapas Bar

Sometimes you just need a bite.
Graze on tapas as you socialize with your companions
or combine several tapas to create a meal.

Restaurant Name:_____

_____

Location:_____

_____

How many in your group?_____

Date Completed:

_____

My Overall Rating:

☆ ☆ ☆ ☆ ☆

What other restaurants did you consider for this challenge?_____

_____

_____

Why did you choose this place over the other possiblities?_____

_____

_____

_____

🍴 Rate The Following

☆☆☆☆☆ Food   ☆☆☆☆☆ Selection

☆☆☆☆☆ Service   ☆☆☆☆☆ Location

☆☆☆☆☆ Cleanliness   ☆☆☆☆☆ Convenience

☆☆☆☆☆ Ambience   ☆☆☆☆☆ Value

What did you order?_____

_____

_____

What other dishes did you consider?_____

_____

_____

Did your order arrive quickly?_____

Were you satisfied with your order? Why or why not?_____

_____

_____

Describe the service you received. Was it fast and friendly? Did

the person helping you seem knowledgable?_____

_____

_____

Describe the atmosphere. Was there anything unique?_____

_____

_____

Would you return to this establishment? Why or why not?_____

_____

_____

Would you like to mention anything else?_____

_____

_____

Not A Chain Or Franchise

Pick whatever restaurant you like for this challenge
as long as it is an independent establishment
and not part of a chain or franchise.

Restaurant Name:_____

_____

Location:_____

_____

How many in your group?_____

Date Completed:

_____

My Overall Rating:

☆☆☆☆☆

What other restaurants did you consider for this challenge?_____

_____

_____

Why did you choose this place over the other possiblities?_____

_____

_____

_____

🍴 Rate The Following

☆☆☆☆☆ Food

☆☆☆☆☆ Service

☆☆☆☆☆ Cleanliness

☆☆☆☆☆ Ambience

☆☆☆☆☆ Selection

☆☆☆☆☆ Location

☆☆☆☆☆ Convenience

☆☆☆☆☆ Value

What did you order?_____

_____

_____

What other dishes did you consider?_____

_____

_____

Did your order arrive quickly?_____

Were you satisfied with your order? Why or why not?____

_____

_____

Describe the service you received. Was it fast and friendly? Did
the person helping you seem knowledgable?_____

_____

_____

Describe the atmosphere. Was there anything unique?_____

_____

_____

Would you return to this establishment? Why or why not?_____

_____

_____

Would you like to mention anything else?_____

_____

_____

A Place That Always Looks Busy

You know the place...the parking lot is regularly full
or there are consistently long lines of eager diners.
Find somewhere that always draws a crowd.

Restaurant Name:_____

_____

Location:_____

_____

How many in your group?_____

Date Completed:

_____

My Overall Rating:

☆☆☆☆☆

What other restaurants did you consider for this challenge?____

_____

_____

Why did you choose this place over the other possiblities?____

_____

_____

_____

🍴 Rate The Following

☆☆☆☆☆ Food   ☆☆☆☆☆ Selection

☆☆☆☆☆ Service   ☆☆☆☆☆ Location

☆☆☆☆☆ Cleanliness   ☆☆☆☆☆ Convenience

☆☆☆☆☆ Ambience   ☆☆☆☆☆ Value

What did you order?_____

_____

What other dishes did you consider?_____

_____

_____

Did your order arrive quickly?_____

Were you satisfied with your order? Why or why not?_____

_____

_____

Describe the service you received. Was it fast and friendly? Did
the person helping you seem knowledgable?_____

_____

_____

Describe the atmosphere. Was there anything unique?_____

_____

_____

Would you return to this establishment? Why or why not?_____

_____

_____

Would you like to mention anything else?_____

_____

_____

A Doughnut Shop

...cake doughnuts...raised doughnuts...filled doughnuts...
...dipped and sprinkled doughnuts...doughnut holes...
...crullers...long johns...glazed doughnuts...

Restaurant Name:_____

_____

Location:_____

_____

How many in your group?_____

Date Completed:

_____

My Overall Rating:

☆☆☆☆☆

What other restaurants did you consider for this challenge?_____

_____

_____

Why did you choose this place over the other possiblities?_____

_____

_____

_____

Rate The Following

☆☆☆☆☆ Food

☆☆☆☆☆ Service

☆☆☆☆☆ Cleanliness

☆☆☆☆☆ Ambience

☆☆☆☆☆ Selection

☆☆☆☆☆ Location

☆☆☆☆☆ Convenience

☆☆☆☆☆ Value

What did you order?_____

_____

_____

What other dishes did you consider?_____

_____

_____

Did your order arrive quickly?_____

Were you satisfied with your order? Why or why not?_____

_____

_____

Describe the service you received. Was it fast and friendly? Did

the person helping you seem knowledgable?_____

_____

_____

Describe the atmosphere. Was there anything unique?_____

_____

_____

Would you return to this establishment? Why or why not?_____

_____

_____

Would you like to mention anything else?_____

_____

_____

Family Style

Affordable, casual dining that is family friendly.
Warm, comfortable and inviting atmosphere with
table service, children's menus, and varying food selections.

Restaurant Name:_____

_____

Location:_____

_____

How many in your group?_____

Date Completed:

_____

My Overall Rating:

☆ ☆ ☆ ☆ ☆

What other restaurants did you consider for this challenge?_____

_____

_____

Why did you choose this place over the other possiblities?_____

_____

_____

_____

🍴 Rate The Following

☆☆☆☆☆ Food   ☆☆☆☆☆ Selection

☆☆☆☆☆ Service   ☆☆☆☆☆ Location

☆☆☆☆☆ Cleanliness   ☆☆☆☆☆ Convenience

☆☆☆☆☆ Ambience   ☆☆☆☆☆ Value

What did you order?_____

_____

_____

What other dishes did you consider?_____

_____

_____

Did your order arrive quickly?_____

Were you satisfied with your order? Why or why not?_____

_____

_____

Describe the service you received. Was it fast and friendly? Did

the person helping you seem knowledgable?_____

_____

_____

Describe the atmosphere. Was there anything unique?_____

_____

_____

Would you return to this establishment? Why or why not?____

_____

_____

Would you like to mention anything else?_____

_____

_____

Buffet

Buffet restaurants can be found serving all types of foods
from pizza and ethnic cuisines to breakfast buffets
and Smörgåsbords. Pick and choose and eat your fill.

Restaurant Name:_____

_____

Location:_____

_____

How many in your group?_____

Date Completed:

_____

My Overall Rating:

☆☆☆☆☆

What other restaurants did you consider for this challenge?_____

_____

_____

Why did you choose this place over the other possiblities?_____

_____

_____

_____

🍴 Rate The Following

☆☆☆☆☆ Food

☆☆☆☆☆ Service

☆☆☆☆☆ Cleanliness

☆☆☆☆☆ Ambience

☆☆☆☆☆ Selection

☆☆☆☆☆ Location

☆☆☆☆☆ Convenience

☆☆☆☆☆ Value

What foods did you have?_____

_____

_____

What other dishes did you consider?_____

_____

_____

Were you satisfied with your meal? Why or why not?_____

_____

_____

_____

Describe the service you received. Was it fast and friendly? Did
the person helping you seem knowledgable?_____

_____

_____

Describe the atmosphere._____

_____

_____

Would you return to this establishment? Why or why not?_____

_____

_____

Would you like to mention anything else?_____

_____

_____

Has A Salad Bar

Find a salad bar and dig in!
Here is your chance to make the perfect salad
with all the toppings you enjoy!

Restaurant Name:_____

_____

Location:_____

_____

How many in your group?_____

Date Completed:
_____
My Overall Rating:
☆ ☆ ☆ ☆ ☆

What other restaurants did you consider for this challenge?_____

_____

_____

Why did you choose this place over the other possiblities?_____

_____

_____

_____

🍴 Rate The Following

☆☆☆☆☆ Food   ☆☆☆☆☆ Selection

☆☆☆☆☆ Service   ☆☆☆☆☆ Location

☆☆☆☆☆ Cleanliness   ☆☆☆☆☆ Convenience

☆☆☆☆☆ Ambience   ☆☆☆☆☆ Value

Did you order anything other than the salad bar? If so, what?

_____

_____

Describe the selection?_____

_____

_____

Were you satisfied with your meal? Why or why not?_____

_____

_____

_____

Describe the service you received. Was it fast and friendly? Did the person helping you seem knowledgable?_____

_____

_____

Describe the atmosphere._____

_____

_____

Would you return to this establishment? Why or why not?_____

_____

_____

Would you like to mention anything else?_____

_____

_____

Their Specialty is Vegetarian or Vegan

A great vegetarian or vegan chef can create dishes
packed with so much delicious flavor,
even meat-eaters will want to eat more veggies!

Restaurant Name:_____

_____

Location:_____

_____

How many in your group?_____

Date Completed:

_____

My Overall Rating:

☆☆☆☆☆

What other restaurants did you consider for this challenge?_____

_____

_____

Why did you choose this place over the other possiblities?_____

_____

_____

_____

🍴 Rate The Following

☆☆☆☆☆ Food   ☆☆☆☆☆ Selection

☆☆☆☆☆ Service   ☆☆☆☆☆ Location

☆☆☆☆☆ Cleanliness   ☆☆☆☆☆ Convenience

☆☆☆☆☆ Ambience   ☆☆☆☆☆ Value

What did you order?_____

_____

_____

What other dishes did you consider?_____

_____

_____

Did your order arrive quickly?_____

Were you satisfied with your order? Why or why not?_____

_____

_____

Describe the service you received. Was it fast and friendly? Did

the person helping you seem knowledgable?_____

_____

_____

Describe the atmosphere. Was there anything unique?_____

_____

_____

Would you return to this establishment? Why or why not?_____

_____

_____

Would you like to mention anything else?_____

_____

_____

Has An Interesting History

Perhaps the building was once an old firehouse, or barn, or hideout during war time. Maybe someone famous once walked through its doors. Find a restaurant an interesting history.

Restaurant Name:_____

_____

Location:_____

_____

How many in your group?_____

Date Completed:

_____

My Overall Rating:

☆ ☆ ☆ ☆ ☆

What other restaurants did you consider for this challenge?_____

_____

_____

Why did you choose this place over the other possiblities?_____

_____

_____

_____

_____

🍴 Rate The Following

☆☆☆☆☆ Food

☆☆☆☆☆ Service

☆☆☆☆☆ Cleanliness

☆☆☆☆☆ Ambience

☆☆☆☆☆ Selection

☆☆☆☆☆ Location

☆☆☆☆☆ Convenience

☆☆☆☆☆ Value

What did you order?_____

_____

_____

What other dishes did you consider?_____

_____

_____

Did your order arrive quickly?_____

Were you satisfied with your order? Why or why not?_____

_____

_____

Describe the service you received. Was it fast and friendly? Did

the person helping you seem knowledgable?_____

_____

_____

Describe the atmosphere. Was there anything unique?_____

_____

_____

Would you return to this establishment? Why or why not?_____

_____

_____

Would you like to mention anything else?_____

_____

_____

A Steakhouse

Choose a restaurant that specializes in steaks and chops
and serves up delicious cuts of meat.
Many will also have poultry and seafood on their menu.

Restaurant Name:_____

_____

Location:_____

_____

How many in your group?_____

Date Completed:

_____

My Overall Rating:

☆☆☆☆☆

What other restaurants did you consider for this challenge?_____

_____

_____

Why did you choose this place over the other possiblities?_____

_____

_____

_____

🍴 Rate The Following

☆☆☆☆☆ Food

☆☆☆☆☆ Service

☆☆☆☆☆ Cleanliness

☆☆☆☆☆ Ambience

☆☆☆☆☆ Selection

☆☆☆☆☆ Location

☆☆☆☆☆ Convenience

☆☆☆☆☆ Value

What did you order?_____

_____

_____

What other dishes did you consider?_____

_____

_____

Did your order arrive quickly?_____

Were you satisfied with your order? Why or why not?_____

_____

_____

Describe the service you received. Was it fast and friendly? Did

the person helping you seem knowledgable?_____

_____

_____

Describe the atmosphere. Was there anything unique?_____

_____

_____

Would you return to this establishment? Why or why not?_____

_____

_____

Would you like to mention anything else?_____

_____

_____

An Ice Cream Parlor

Try some creamy soft serve or an indulgent banana split.
Whether they have a wide variety of flavors or
a small selection of hand-churned specialties, enjoy!

Restaurant Name:_____

_____

Location:_____

_____

How many in your group?_____

Date Completed:

_____

My Overall Rating:

☆☆☆☆☆

What other restaurants did you consider for this challenge?_____

_____

_____

Why did you choose this place over the other possiblities?_____

_____

_____

_____

🍴 Rate The Following

☆☆☆☆☆ Food

☆☆☆☆☆ Service

☆☆☆☆☆ Cleanliness

☆☆☆☆☆ Ambience

☆☆☆☆☆ Selection

☆☆☆☆☆ Location

☆☆☆☆☆ Convenience

☆☆☆☆☆ Value

What did you order?_____

_____

_____

What other dishes did you consider?_____

_____

_____

Did your order arrive quickly?_____

Were you satisfied with your order? Why or why not?_____

_____

_____

Describe the service you received. Was it fast and friendly? Did
the person helping you seem knowledgable?_____

_____

_____

Describe the atmosphere. Was there anything unique?_____

_____

_____

Would you return to this establishment? Why or why not?_____

_____

_____

Would you like to mention anything else?_____

_____

_____

Dinner Theater

Choose a live mystery show or a small, intimate music concert.
Perhaps a comedy act, a play, or simply a movie
Find some entertainment to enjoy while you dine.

Restaurant Name:_____

_____

Location:_____

_____

How many in your group?_____

Date Completed:

_____

My Overall Rating:

☆☆☆☆☆

What other restaurants did you consider for this challenge?_____

_____

_____

Why did you choose this place over the other possiblities?_____

_____

_____

_____

🍴 Rate The Following

☆☆☆☆☆ Food

☆☆☆☆☆ Service

☆☆☆☆☆ Cleanliness

☆☆☆☆☆ Ambience

☆☆☆☆☆ Selection

☆☆☆☆☆ Location

☆☆☆☆☆ Convenience

☆☆☆☆☆ Value

What did you order?_____

_____

_____

What other dishes did you consider?_____

_____

_____

Did your order arrive quickly?_____

Were you satisfied with your order? Why or why not?_____

_____

_____

Describe the service you received. Was it fast and friendly? Did
the person helping you seem knowledgable?_____

_____

_____

What type of entertainment was there?_____

_____

_____

Would you return to this establishment? Why or why not?_____

_____

_____

Would you like to mention anything else?_____

_____

_____

A Pizzeria

Locate a pizzeria and sit down to one of the
most popular dishes in the world...pizza. Enjoy the
dine-in experience and save the delivery for another day.

Restaurant Name:_____

_____

Location:_____

_____

How many in your group?_____

Date Completed:

_____

My Overall Rating:

☆☆☆☆☆

What other restaurants did you consider for this challenge?_____

_____

_____

Why did you choose this place over the other possiblities?_____

_____

_____

_____

🍴 Rate The Following

☆☆☆☆☆ Food

☆☆☆☆☆ Service

☆☆☆☆☆ Cleanliness

☆☆☆☆☆ Ambience

☆☆☆☆☆ Selection

☆☆☆☆☆ Location

☆☆☆☆☆ Convenience

☆☆☆☆☆ Value

What did you order?_____

_____

_____

What other dishes did you consider?_____

_____

_____

Did your order arrive quickly?_____

Were you satisfied with your order? Why or why not?_____

_____

_____

Describe the service you received. Was it fast and friendly? Did

the person helping you seem knowledgable?_____

_____

_____

Describe the atmosphere. Was there anything unique?_____

_____

_____

Would you return to this establishment? Why or why not?_____

_____

_____

Would you like to mention anything else?_____

_____

_____

Fast Casual

Enjoy the convenience of a fast food restaurant
paired with the ambiance and food quality
of a casual dining restaurant.

Restaurant Name:_____

_____

Location:_____

_____

How many in your group?_____

Date Completed:

_____

My Overall Rating:

☆☆☆☆☆

What other restaurants did you consider for this challenge?_____

_____

_____

Why did you choose this place over the other possiblities?_____

_____

_____

_____

🍴 Rate The Following

☆☆☆☆☆ Food   ☆☆☆☆☆ Selection

☆☆☆☆☆ Service   ☆☆☆☆☆ Location

☆☆☆☆☆ Cleanliness   ☆☆☆☆☆ Convenience

☆☆☆☆☆ Ambience   ☆☆☆☆☆ Value

What did you order?_____

_____

_____

What other dishes did you consider?_____

_____

_____

Did your order arrive quickly?_____

Were you satisfied with your order? Why or why not?_____

_____

_____

Describe the service you received. Was it fast and friendly? Did

the person helping you seem knowledgable?_____

_____

_____

Describe the atmosphere. Was there anything unique?_____

_____

_____

Would you return to this establishment? Why or why not?_____

_____

_____

Would you like to mention anything else?_____

_____

_____

Teahouse

Teahouses or tea rooms can vary widely in ambience and offerings (Asian vs. European) but will usually have a variety of teas and a selection of light dishes or pastries.

Restaurant Name:_____

_____

Location:_____

_____

How many in your group?_____

Date Completed:

_____

My Overall Rating:

☆☆☆☆☆

What other restaurants did you consider for this challenge?_____

_____

_____

Why did you choose this place over the other possiblities?_____

_____

_____

_____

🍴 Rate The Following

☆☆☆☆☆ Food

☆☆☆☆☆ Service

☆☆☆☆☆ Cleanliness

☆☆☆☆☆ Ambience

☆☆☆☆☆ Selection

☆☆☆☆☆ Location

☆☆☆☆☆ Convenience

☆☆☆☆☆ Value

What did you order?_____

_____

_____

What other dishes did you consider?_____

_____

_____

Did your order arrive quickly?_____

Were you satisfied with your order? Why or why not?_____

_____

_____

Describe the service you received. Was it fast and friendly? Did

the person helping you seem knowledgable?_____

_____

_____

Describe the atmosphere. Was there anything unique?_____

_____

_____

Would you return to this establishment? Why or why not?_____

_____

_____

Would you like to mention anything else?_____

_____

_____

Place You've Been Wanting To Try

You've probably had your eye on a restaurant.
Here's your chance to give it a try!
Bon appétit!

Restaurant Name:_____

_____

Location:_____

_____

How many in your group?_____

Date Completed:

_____

My Overall Rating:

☆ ☆ ☆ ☆ ☆

What other restaurants did you consider for this challenge?_____

_____

_____

Why did you choose this place over the other possiblities?_____

_____

_____

_____

_____

🍴 Rate The Following

☆☆☆☆☆ Food   ☆☆☆☆☆ Selection

☆☆☆☆☆ Service   ☆☆☆☆☆ Location

☆☆☆☆☆ Cleanliness   ☆☆☆☆☆ Convenience

☆☆☆☆☆ Ambience   ☆☆☆☆☆ Value

What did you order?_____

_____

_____

What other dishes did you consider?_____

_____

_____

Did your order arrive quickly?_____

Were you satisfied with your order? Why or why not?_____

_____

_____

Describe the service you received. Was it fast and friendly? Did

the person helping you seem knowledgable?_____

_____

_____

Describe the atmosphere. Was there anything unique?_____

_____

_____

Would you return to this establishment? Why or why not?_____

_____

_____

Would you like to mention anything else?_____

_____

_____

Challenge #34

Sushi Bar

Try to find a sushi bar
where you can interact with your sushi chef
and watch them in action.

Restaurant Name:_____

_____

Location:_____

_____

How many in your group?_____

Date Completed:

_____

My Overall Rating:

☆☆☆☆☆

What other restaurants did you consider for this challenge?_____

_____

_____

Why did you choose this place over the other possiblities?_____

_____

_____

_____

Rate The Following

☆☆☆☆☆ Food

☆☆☆☆☆ Service

☆☆☆☆☆ Cleanliness

☆☆☆☆☆ Ambience

☆☆☆☆☆ Selection

☆☆☆☆☆ Location

☆☆☆☆☆ Convenience

☆☆☆☆☆ Value

What did you order?_____

_____

_____

What other dishes did you consider?_____

_____

_____

Did your order arrive quickly?_____

Were you satisfied with your order? Why or why not?_____

_____

_____

Describe the service you received. Was it fast and friendly? Did

the person helping you seem knowledgable?_____

_____

_____

Describe the atmosphere. Was there anything unique?_____

_____

_____

Would you return to this establishment? Why or why not?_____

_____

_____

Would you like to mention anything else?_____

_____

_____

Challenge #35

Their Specialty Is Bread

Breads baked fresh daily...mmmm!
Usually these establishments are bakeries or sandwich shops.
Take some baked deliciousness home with you if you can!

Restaurant Name:_____

_____

Location:_____

_____

How many in your group?_____

Date Completed:

_____

My Overall Rating:

☆☆☆☆☆

What other restaurants did you consider for this challenge?_____

_____

_____

Why did you choose this place over the other possiblities?_____

_____

_____

_____

🍴 Rate The Following

☆☆☆☆☆ Food   ☆☆☆☆☆ Selection

☆☆☆☆☆ Service   ☆☆☆☆☆ Location

☆☆☆☆☆ Cleanliness ☆☆☆☆☆ Convenience

☆☆☆☆☆ Ambience   ☆☆☆☆☆ Value

What did you order?_____

_____

_____

What other dishes did you consider?_____

_____

_____

Did your order arrive quickly?_____

Were you satisfied with your order? Why or why not?_____

_____

_____

Describe the service you received. Was it fast and friendly? Did

the person helping you seem knowledgable?_____

_____

_____

Describe the atmosphere. Was there anything unique?_____

_____

_____

Would you return to this establishment? Why or why not?_____

_____

_____

Would you like to mention anything else?_____

_____

_____

Fine Dining

Dress up and show off your finest table manners!
This challenge can be used for the most special occasions.
Enjoy fine foods in a formal setting.

Restaurant Name:_____

_____

Location:_____

_____

How many in your group?_____

Date Completed:

_____

My Overall Rating:

☆ ☆ ☆ ☆ ☆

What other restaurants did you consider for this challenge?_____

_____

_____

Why did you choose this place over the other possiblities?_____

_____

_____

_____

🍴 Rate The Following

☆☆☆☆☆ Food   ☆☆☆☆☆ Selection

☆☆☆☆☆ Service   ☆☆☆☆☆ Location

☆☆☆☆☆ Cleanliness   ☆☆☆☆☆ Convenience

☆☆☆☆☆ Ambience   ☆☆☆☆☆ Value

What did you order?_____

_____

_____

What other dishes did you consider?_____

_____

_____

Did your order arrive quickly?_____

Were you satisfied with your order? Why or why not?_____

_____

_____

Describe the service you received. Was it fast and friendly? Did

the person helping you seem knowledgable?_____

_____

_____

Describe the atmosphere. Was there anything unique?_____

_____

_____

Would you return to this establishment? Why or why not?_____

_____

_____

Would you like to mention anything else?_____

_____

_____

A Delicatessen (Deli)

Your experience will depend on your location. You may find
gourmet foods and delicacies, ethnic selections, or
a variety of hot & cold dishes and made to order sandwiches.

Restaurant Name:_____

_____

Location:_____

_____

How many in your group?_____

Date Completed:

_____

My Overall Rating:

☆☆☆☆☆

What other restaurants did you consider for this challenge?_____

_____

_____

Why did you choose this place over the other possiblities?_____

_____

_____

_____

🍴 Rate The Following

☆☆☆☆☆ Food

☆☆☆☆☆ Service

☆☆☆☆☆ Cleanliness

☆☆☆☆☆ Ambience

☆☆☆☆☆ Selection

☆☆☆☆☆ Location

☆☆☆☆☆ Convenience

☆☆☆☆☆ Value

What did you order?_____

_____

_____

What other dishes did you consider?_____

_____

_____

Did your order arrive quickly?_____

Were you satisfied with your order? Why or why not?_____

_____

_____

Describe the service you received. Was it fast and friendly? Did

the person helping you seem knowledgable?_____

_____

_____

Describe the atmosphere. Was there anything unique?_____

_____

_____

Would you return to this establishment? Why or why not?_____

_____

_____

Would you like to mention anything else?_____

_____

_____

Named After A Person

Choose a restaurant that is named after a person.
It might be named after
the owner, the chef, or even a celebrity.

Restaurant Name:_____

_____

Location:_____

_____

How many in your group?_____

Date Completed:

_____

My Overall Rating:

☆☆☆☆☆

What other restaurants did you consider for this challenge?_____

_____

_____

Why did you choose this place over the other possiblities?_____

_____

_____

_____

_____

🍴 Rate The Following

☆☆☆☆☆ Food   ☆☆☆☆☆ Selection

☆☆☆☆☆ Service   ☆☆☆☆☆ Location

☆☆☆☆☆ Cleanliness   ☆☆☆☆☆ Convenience

☆☆☆☆☆ Ambience   ☆☆☆☆☆ Value

What did you order?_____

_____

_____

What other dishes did you consider?_____

_____

_____

Did your order arrive quickly?_____

Were you satisfied with your order? Why or why not?_____

_____

_____

Describe the service you received. Was it fast and friendly? Did
the person helping you seem knowledgable?_____

_____

_____

Describe the atmosphere. Was there anything unique?_____

_____

_____

Would you return to this establishment? Why or why not?_____

_____

_____

Would you like to mention anything else?_____

_____

_____

Street Food

As food cart and food truck numbers increase, their menus are becoming more varied offering everything from the usual hot dogs & burgers to the unexpected sushi, fry bread, and lobster!

Restaurant Name:_____

_____

Location:_____

_____

How many in your group?_____

Date Completed:

_____

My Overall Rating:

☆☆☆☆☆

What other restaurants did you consider for this challenge?____

_____

_____

Why did you choose this place over the other possiblities?____

_____

_____

_____

🍴 Rate The Following

☆☆☆☆☆ Food   ☆☆☆☆☆ Selection

☆☆☆☆☆ Service   ☆☆☆☆☆ Location

☆☆☆☆☆ Cleanliness   ☆☆☆☆☆ Convenience

☆☆☆☆☆ Ambience   ☆☆☆☆☆ Value

What did you order?_____

_____

_____

What other dishes did you consider?_____

_____

_____

Did your order arrive quickly?_____

Were you satisfied with your order? Why or why not?_____

_____

_____

Describe the service you received. Was it fast and friendly? Did

the person helping you seem knowledgable?_____

_____

_____

Describe the atmosphere. Was there anything unique?_____

_____

_____

Would you return to this establishment? Why or why not?_____

_____

_____

Would you like to mention anything else?_____

_____

_____

Their Specialty Is Breakfast

Pancakes, waffles, biscuits or a breakfast buffet...
whether they have limited breakfast hours or they serve
breakfast all day, the first meal of the day is their specialty.

Restaurant Name:_____

_____

Location:_____

_____

How many in your group?_____

Date Completed:

_____

My Overall Rating:

☆☆☆☆☆

What other restaurants did you consider for this challenge?_____

_____

_____

Why did you choose this place over the other possiblities?_____

_____

_____

_____

🍴 Rate The Following

☆☆☆☆☆ Food

☆☆☆☆☆ Service

☆☆☆☆☆ Cleanliness

☆☆☆☆☆ Ambience

☆☆☆☆☆ Selection

☆☆☆☆☆ Location

☆☆☆☆☆ Convenience

☆☆☆☆☆ Value

What did you order?_____

_____

_____

What other dishes did you consider?_____

_____

_____

Did your order arrive quickly?_____

Were you satisfied with your order? Why or why not?_____

_____

_____

Describe the service you received. Was it fast and friendly? Did

the person helping you seem knowledgable?_____

_____

_____

Describe the atmosphere. Was there anything unique?_____

_____

_____

Would you return to this establishment? Why or why not?_____

_____

_____

Would you like to mention anything else?_____

_____

_____

A Bakery

Flaky pastries, mouthwatering muffins, fresh breads
and tempting doughnuts...it may be hard
to choose just one thing at a bakery.

Restaurant Name:_____

_____

Location:_____

_____

How many in your group?_____

Date Completed:

_____

My Overall Rating:

☆ ☆ ☆ ☆ ☆

What other restaurants did you consider for this challenge?_____

_____

_____

Why did you choose this place over the other possiblities?_____

_____

_____

_____

🍴 Rate The Following

☆☆☆☆☆ Food   ☆☆☆☆☆ Selection

☆☆☆☆☆ Service   ☆☆☆☆☆ Location

☆☆☆☆☆ Cleanliness   ☆☆☆☆☆ Convenience

☆☆☆☆☆ Ambience   ☆☆☆☆☆ Value

What did you order?_____

_____

_____

What other dishes did you consider?_____

_____

_____

Did your order arrive quickly?_____

Were you satisfied with your order? Why or why not?_____

_____

_____

Describe the service you received. Was it fast and friendly? Did
the person helping you seem knowledgable?_____

_____

_____

Describe the atmosphere. Was there anything unique?_____

_____

_____

Would you return to this establishment? Why or why not?_____

_____

_____

Would you like to mention anything else?_____

_____

_____

Combined Food & Activity

Take a cooking class. Enjoy dinner and bowling.
Stroll through a street fair while sampling a variety of treats.
Find an activity and combine it with food.

Restaurant Name:_____

_____

Location:_____

_____

How many in your group?_____

Date Completed:

_____

My Overall Rating:

☆☆☆☆☆

What other restaurants did you consider for this challenge?_____

_____

_____

Why did you choose this place over the other possiblities?_____

_____

_____

_____

🍴 Rate The Following

☆☆☆☆☆ Food

☆☆☆☆☆ Service

☆☆☆☆☆ Cleanliness

☆☆☆☆☆ Ambience

☆☆☆☆☆ Selection

☆☆☆☆☆ Location

☆☆☆☆☆ Convenience

☆☆☆☆☆ Value

What did you order?_____

_____

_____

What other dishes did you consider?_____

_____

_____

Were you satisfied with your order? Why or why not?_____

_____

_____

_____

Describe the service you received. Was it fast and friendly? Did
the person helping you seem knowledgable?_____

_____

_____

Describe the atmosphere._____

_____

_____

Would you return to this establishment? Why or why not?_____

_____

_____

Would you like to mention anything else?_____

_____

_____

A Great Place For Groups

Find a great spot that will comfortably accommodate a group.
Dine with family, friends, or even
a bunch of co-workers or neighbors.

Restaurant Name:_____

_____

Location:_____

_____

How many in your group?_____

Date Completed:
_____
My Overall Rating:
☆ ☆ ☆ ☆ ☆

What other restaurants did you consider for this challenge?____

_____

_____

Why did you choose this place over the other possiblities?____

_____

_____

_____

🍴 Rate The Following

☆☆☆☆☆ Food   ☆☆☆☆☆ Selection

☆☆☆☆☆ Service   ☆☆☆☆☆ Location

☆☆☆☆☆ Cleanliness   ☆☆☆☆☆ Convenience

☆☆☆☆☆ Ambience   ☆☆☆☆☆ Value

What did you order?_____

_____

_____

What other dishes did you consider?_____

_____

_____

Did your order arrive quickly?_____

Were you satisfied with your order? Why or why not?_____

_____

_____

Describe the service you received. Was it fast and friendly? Did
the person helping you seem knowledgable?_____

_____

_____

Describe the atmosphere. Was there anything unique?_____

_____

_____

Would you return to this establishment? Why or why not?_____

_____

_____

Would you like to mention anything else?_____

_____

_____

Challenge #44

A Cafeteria

Some areas have stand-alone cafeterias,
but most cafeterias can be found in places like
schools and businesses.

Restaurant Name:_____

_____

Location:_____

_____

How many in your group?_____

Date Completed:

_____

My Overall Rating:

☆☆☆☆☆

What other cafeterias did you consider for this challenge?_____

_____

_____

Why did you choose this place over the other possiblities?_____

_____

_____

_____

Rate The Following

☆☆☆☆☆ Food

☆☆☆☆☆ Service

☆☆☆☆☆ Cleanliness

☆☆☆☆☆ Ambience

☆☆☆☆☆ Selection

☆☆☆☆☆ Location

☆☆☆☆☆ Convenience

☆☆☆☆☆ Value

What did you order?_____

_____

_____

What other dishes did you consider?_____

_____

_____

Were you satisfied with your order? Why or why not?_____

_____

_____

_____

Describe the service you received. Was it fast and friendly? Did

the person helping you seem knowledgable?_____

_____

_____

Describe the atmosphere._____

_____

_____

Would you return to this establishment? Why or why not?____

_____

_____

Would you like to mention anything else?_____

_____

_____

Challenge #45

Their Specialty Is Barbecue

The smell of the smoker will have you following your nose to a great barbecue spot. Barbecue varies greatly by region and each claims their version is the best. Better try them all.

Restaurant Name:_____

_____

Location:_____

_____

How many in your group?_____

Date Completed:

_____

My Overall Rating:

☆☆☆☆☆

What other restaurants did you consider for this challenge?____

_____

_____

Why did you choose this place over the other possiblities?_____

_____

_____

_____

_____

🍴 Rate The Following

☆☆☆☆☆ Food

☆☆☆☆☆ Service

☆☆☆☆☆ Cleanliness

☆☆☆☆☆ Ambience

☆☆☆☆☆ Selection

☆☆☆☆☆ Location

☆☆☆☆☆ Convenience

☆☆☆☆☆ Value

What did you order?_____

_____

_____

What other dishes did you consider?_____

_____

_____

Did your order arrive quickly?_____

Were you satisfied with your order? Why or why not?_____

_____

_____

Describe the service you received. Was it fast and friendly? Did

the person helping you seem knowledgable?_____

_____

_____

Describe the atmosphere. Was there anything unique?_____

_____

_____

Would you return to this establishment? Why or why not?_____

_____

_____

Would you like to mention anything else?_____

_____

_____

Pop-Up Restaurant

You will probably need to do some homework to find one of these temporary restaurants in your area, but it may give you a chance to discover a new chef or dining concept.

Restaurant Name:_____

_____

Location:_____

_____

How many in your group?_____

Date Completed:

_____

My Overall Rating:

☆☆☆☆☆

What other restaurants did you consider for this challenge?_____

_____

_____

Why did you choose this place over the other possiblities?_____

_____

_____

_____

🍴 Rate The Following

☆☆☆☆☆ Food

☆☆☆☆☆ Service

☆☆☆☆☆ Cleanliness

☆☆☆☆☆ Ambience

☆☆☆☆☆ Selection

☆☆☆☆☆ Location

☆☆☆☆☆ Convenience

☆☆☆☆☆ Value

What did you order?_____

_____

_____

What other dishes did you consider?_____

_____

_____

Did your order arrive quickly?_____

Were you satisfied with your order? Why or why not?_____

_____

_____

Describe the service you received. Was it fast and friendly? Did
the person helping you seem knowledgable?_____

_____

_____

Describe the atmosphere. Was there anything unique?_____

_____

_____

Would you like to see this pop-up become permanent?_____

_____

_____

Would you like to mention anything else?_____

_____

_____

A Diner

Diners may not all have 50s style retro tables and cushioned stools, but they do all typically serve favorites like burgers and shakes or homestyle meals.

Restaurant Name:_____

_____

Location:_____

_____

How many in your group?_____

Date Completed:

_____

My Overall Rating:

☆☆☆☆☆

What other restaurants did you consider for this challenge?_____

_____

_____

Why did you choose this place over the other possiblities?_____

_____

_____

_____

_____

🍴 Rate The Following

☆☆☆☆☆ Food

☆☆☆☆☆ Service

☆☆☆☆☆ Cleanliness

☆☆☆☆☆ Ambience

☆☆☆☆☆ Selection

☆☆☆☆☆ Location

☆☆☆☆☆ Convenience

☆☆☆☆☆ Value

What did you order?_____

_____

_____

What other dishes did you consider?_____

_____

_____

Did your order arrive quickly?_____

Were you satisfied with your order? Why or why not?_____

_____

_____

Describe the service you received. Was it fast and friendly? Did
the person helping you seem knowledgable?_____

_____

_____

Describe the atmosphere. Was there anything unique?_____

_____

_____

Would you return to this establishment? Why or why not?_____

_____

_____

Would you like to mention anything else?_____

_____

_____

A Beer Garden

Enjoy a selection of beer, food,
and sometimes entertainment,
in an outdoor space.

Restaurant Name:_____

_____

Location:_____

_____

How many in your group?_____

Date Completed:

_____

My Overall Rating:

☆☆☆☆☆

What other restaurants did you consider for this challenge?_____

_____

_____

Why did you choose this place over the other possiblities?_____

_____

_____

_____

🍴 Rate The Following

☆☆☆☆☆ Food

☆☆☆☆☆ Service

☆☆☆☆☆ Cleanliness

☆☆☆☆☆ Ambience

☆☆☆☆☆ Selection

☆☆☆☆☆ Location

☆☆☆☆☆ Convenience

☆☆☆☆☆ Value

What did you order?_____

_____

_____

What other dishes did you consider?_____

_____

_____

Did your order arrive quickly?_____

Were you satisfied with your order? Why or why not?_____

_____

_____

Describe the service you received. Was it fast and friendly? Did
the person helping you seem knowledgable?_____

_____

_____

Describe the atmosphere. Was there anything unique?_____

_____

_____

Would you return to this establishment? Why or why not?_____

_____

_____

Would you like to mention anything else?_____

_____

_____

Sandwich Shop

Whether you choose a panini with gooey cheese, a club piled high with tasty bits, or a sub made your way from a sandwich bar, sometimes a sandwich just hits the spot.

Restaurant Name:_____

_____

Location:_____

_____

How many in your group?_____

Date Completed:

_____

My Overall Rating:

☆☆☆☆☆

What other restaurants did you consider for this challenge?_____

_____

_____

Why did you choose this place over the other possiblities?_____

_____

_____

_____

🍴 Rate The Following

☆☆☆☆☆ Food

☆☆☆☆☆ Service

☆☆☆☆☆ Cleanliness

☆☆☆☆☆ Ambience

☆☆☆☆☆ Selection

☆☆☆☆☆ Location

☆☆☆☆☆ Convenience

☆☆☆☆☆ Value

What did you order?_____

_____

_____

What other dishes did you consider?_____

_____

_____

Did your order arrive quickly?_____

Were you satisfied with your order? Why or why not?_____

_____

_____

Describe the service you received. Was it fast and friendly? Did
the person helping you seem knowledgable?_____

_____

_____

Describe the atmosphere. Was there anything unique?_____

_____

_____

Would you return to this establishment? Why or why not?_____

_____

_____

Would you like to mention anything else?_____.

_____

_____

Challenge #50

Reservations Recommended

You could be off to a popular spot for a fancy date
or celebrating a special occasion. Either way, don't forget
to make those reservations ahead of time!

Restaurant Name:_____

_____

Location:_____

_____

How many in your group?_____

Date Completed:

_____

My Overall Rating:

☆☆☆☆☆

What other restaurants did you consider for this challenge?____

_____

_____

Why did you choose this place over the other possiblities?____

_____

_____

_____

🍴 Rate The Following

☆☆☆☆☆ Food　　☆☆☆☆☆ Selection

☆☆☆☆☆ Service　　☆☆☆☆☆ Location

☆☆☆☆☆ Cleanliness　　☆☆☆☆☆ Convenience

☆☆☆☆☆ Ambience　　☆☆☆☆☆ Value

What did you order?_____

_____

_____

What other dishes did you consider?_____

_____

_____

Did your order arrive quickly?_____

Were you satisfied with your order? Why or why not?_____

_____

_____

Describe the service you received. Was it fast and friendly? Did
the person helping you seem knowledgable?_____

_____

_____

Describe the atmosphere. Was there anything unique?_____

_____

_____

Would you return to this establishment? Why or why not?_____

_____

_____

Would you like to mention anything else?_____

_____

_____

Challenge #51

A Gastropub

While they still offer an assortment of beverages,
the gastropub is more of a pub/restaurant hybrid
and focuses on high-quality, flavorful food.

Restaurant Name:_____

Location:_____

How many in your group?_____

Date Completed:
_____

My Overall Rating:
☆☆☆☆☆

What other restaurants did you consider for this challenge?_____

_____

_____

Why did you choose this place over the other possiblities?_____

_____

_____

_____

_____

🍴 Rate The Following

☆☆☆☆☆ Food

☆☆☆☆☆ Service

☆☆☆☆☆ Cleanliness

☆☆☆☆☆ Ambience

☆☆☆☆☆ Selection

☆☆☆☆☆ Location

☆☆☆☆☆ Convenience

☆☆☆☆☆ Value

What did you order?_____

_____

_____

What other dishes did you consider?_____

_____

_____

Did your order arrive quickly?_____

Were you satisfied with your order? Why or why not?_____

_____

_____

Describe the service you received. Was it fast and friendly? Did

the person helping you seem knowledgable?_____

_____

_____

Describe the atmosphere. Was there anything unique?_____

_____

_____

Would you return to this establishment? Why or why not?_____

_____

_____

Would you like to mention anything else?_____

_____

_____

Challenge #52

Your Favorite Restaurant

If you have more than one favorite restaurant,
the challenge here will be to choose only one.

Restaurant Name:_____

_____

Location:_____

_____

How many in your group?_____

Date Completed:

_____

My Overall Rating:

☆ ☆ ☆ ☆ ☆

What other restaurants did you consider for this challenge?_____

_____

_____

Why did you choose this place over the other possiblities?_____

_____

_____

_____

_____

🍴 Rate The Following

☆☆☆☆☆ Food

☆☆☆☆☆ Service

☆☆☆☆☆ Cleanliness

☆☆☆☆☆ Ambience

☆☆☆☆☆ Selection

☆☆☆☆☆ Location

☆☆☆☆☆ Convenience

☆☆☆☆☆ Value

How often do you visit this restaurant?_____

_____

_____

What dishes do you recommend?_____

_____

_____

Describe the staff and service._____

_____

_____

_____

Describe the atmosphere._____

_____

_____

_____

What keep you coming back to this restaurant? The food,

service, atmosphere, or a combination?_____

_____

_____

_____

_____

Would you like to mention anything else?_____

_____

_____

Printed in Great Britain
by Amazon